Making Wooden Boxes with Dale Power

Text written with and photography by Jeffrey B. Snyder

Schiffer Publishing Ltd
4880 Lower Valley Road, Atglen, PA 19310 USA

Contents

Library of Congress Catalog Card Number:99-60109

Book Designed by Randy L. Hensley

Type set in Americana XBd BT heading font/text font Humanist 521 BT

ISBN: 0-7643-0848-3

Printed in China

Published by Schiffer Publishing Ltd.
4880 Lower Valley Road
Atglen, PA 19310
Phone: (610) 593-1777; Fax: (610) 593-2002
E-mail: Schifferbk@aol.com
Please visit our web site catalog at
www.schifferbooks.com

This book may be purchased from the publisher.
Include $3.95 for shipping.
Please try your bookstore first.
We are interested in hearing from authors
with book ideas on related subjects.
You may write for a free catalog.

In Europe, Schiffer books are distributed by
Bushwood Books
6 Marksbury Rd.
Kew Gardens
Surrey TW9 4JF England
Phone: 44 (0)181 392-8585; Fax: 44 (0)181 392-9876
E-mail: Bushwd@aol.com

Please try your bookstore first.

Introduction

This book will present you with a variety of box making techniques. The projects range from the simple to the complex. The techniques necessary for creating simple band saw boxes are discussed first. The projects become more complex as we continue, exploring a variety of different joints available to box makers, including mitered cornered, rabbet, spline, and false spline joints. Instructions for successfully cutting loose lids and hinging them are also provided. Following the discussion of box assembly, we will examine several different ways to finish the boxes you make. I hope you enjoy these projects.

—Dale Power

Tools

Tools needed to create and complete the box projects presented here include: a band saw, a table saw, a planer and jointer are helpful if your wood is not perfectly straight, a wood shaper, a dado head, a flush cutting saw, glues (spray adhesive, instant glue, gap filler glue, and yellow carpenter's glue), an instant accelerator for the instant glue, sandpaper (a hand sander, a disk sander, and a belt sander can speed up the sanding process), clamps, an awl, 45 degree and right triangles, razor blades or a utility knife, a pencil, masking tape, small hinges, drawer pull knobs, and small felt pads.

To finish the boxes, you will need:
felt, clear wood finish (spray on), paint rollers, stains and sealers, gold antique glaze, and finishing wax.

Projects
Cutting & Assembling the Boxes

Band Saw Boxes

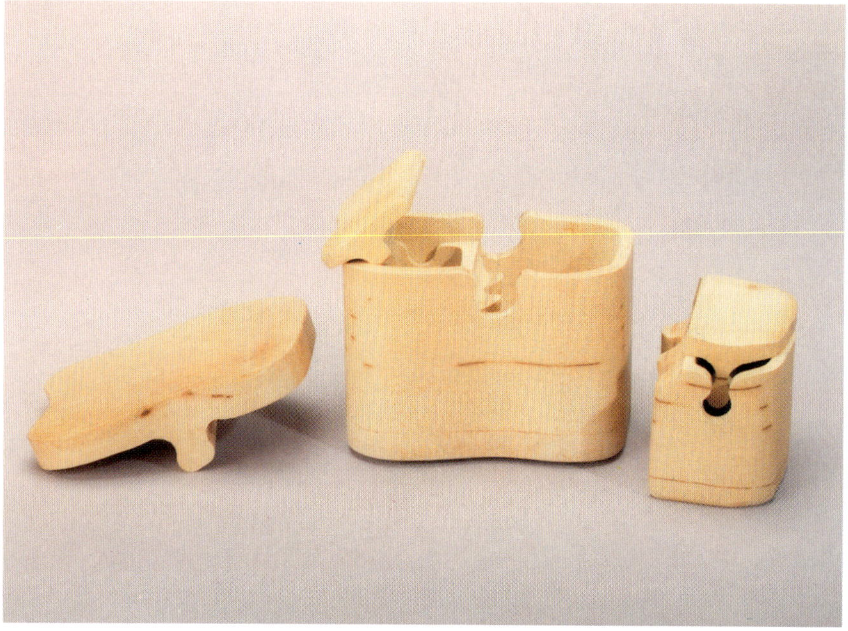

The first band saw box.

We are going to fashion this scrap piece of wood into a band saw box. First shape the outside of the box.

The outside of the box has been roughly shaped with the band saw.

Draw a guide line, indicating where the bottom of the box will be cut off.

Draw in witness marks on both the top and the bottom guide lines to assure that you be able to reorient the lid and base correctly when you reassemble them.

Cut away the base.

Draw in the top of the box as well with any kind of a fancy cut you would like to make. Remember, however, that the blade you are using can only cut a radius that is twice its own width (i.e. a 3/16" blade will make a 3/8" radius cut).

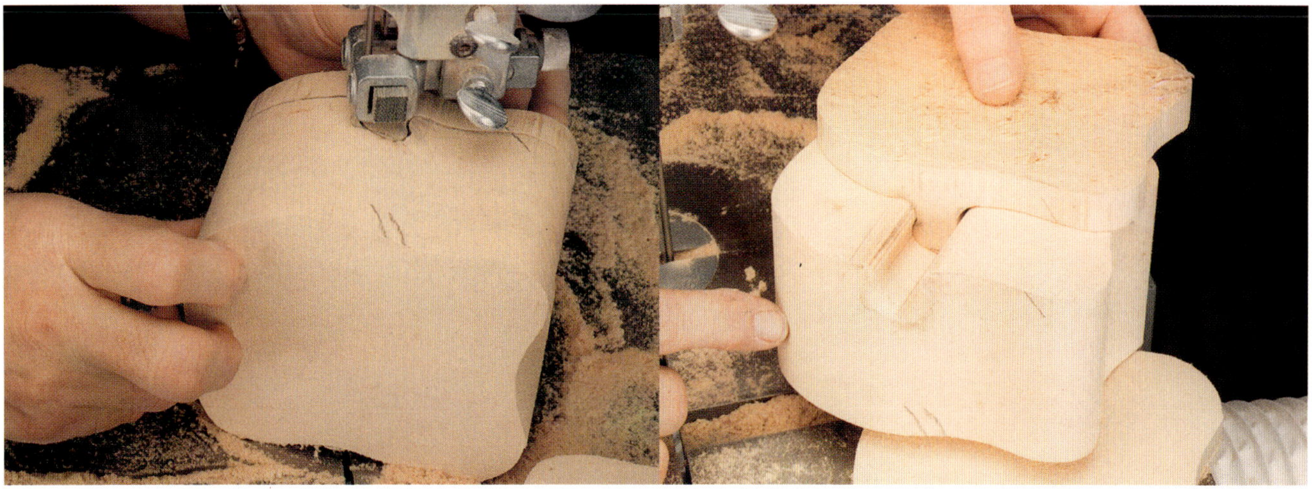

Cut the box top and bottom loose with the band saw.

Using your finger as a guide, draw in the line that represents the inside edge of the box.

Cut along the inside guide lines.

Cut into the back of the box with your saw blade. Make your interior cuts small to ensure that you can make as tight a circle as possible within the box.

Remove the center. Clean up along the back inside edge of the box where the saw blade would not follow the guide lines precisely. This will make the inside edge of the box uniform.

This is an instant gap filler glue that works very well when sealing the joint created along the back edge of the box by the band saw.

Spray the joint with instant accelerator along one side of the joint...

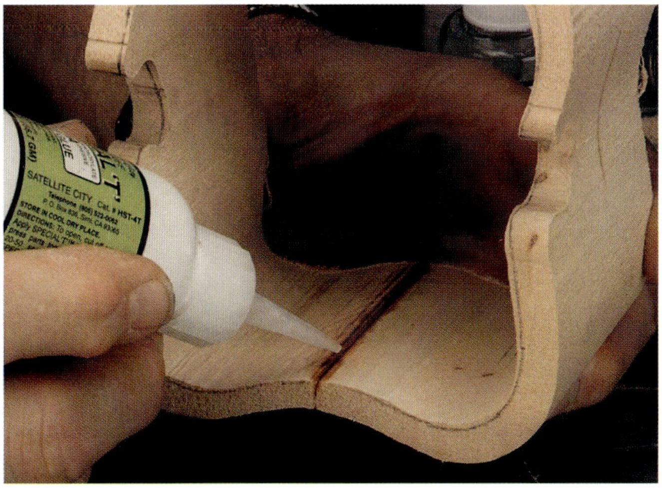

and apply the instant glue to the other side of the joint.

Now lightly sand the inside of the bottom edge to remove any loose fibers.

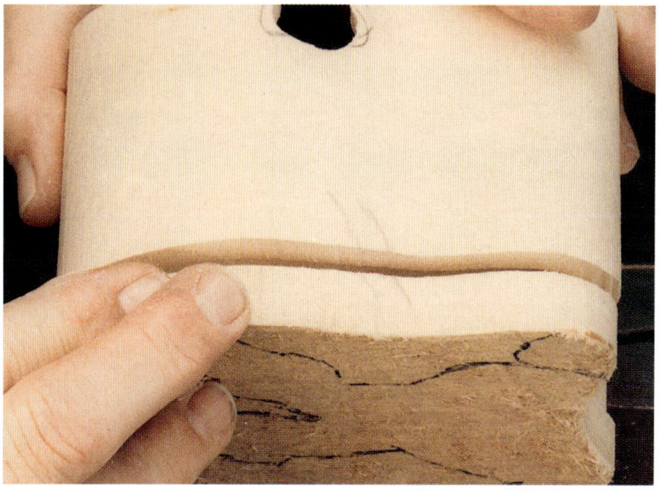

Check to make sure that the witness marks match up along the base now.

Apply the instant glue to the lower edge of the box body ...

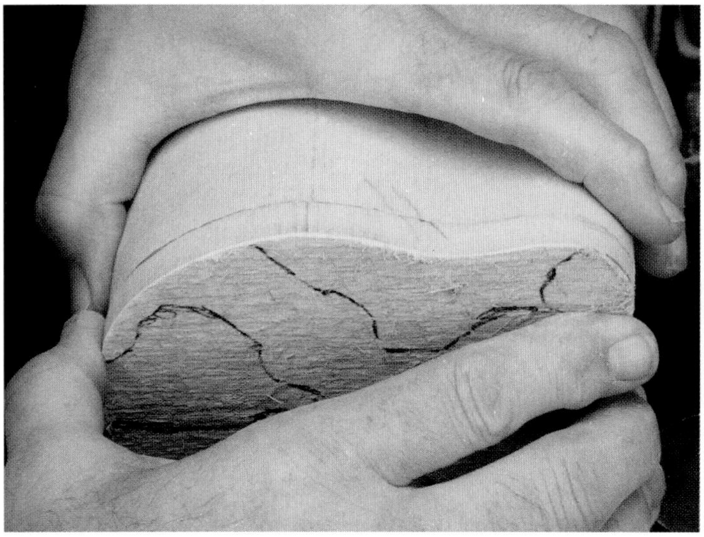

and then apply the accelerator to the base and join the two pieces together. You may wish to apply additional accelerator to the joined seam.

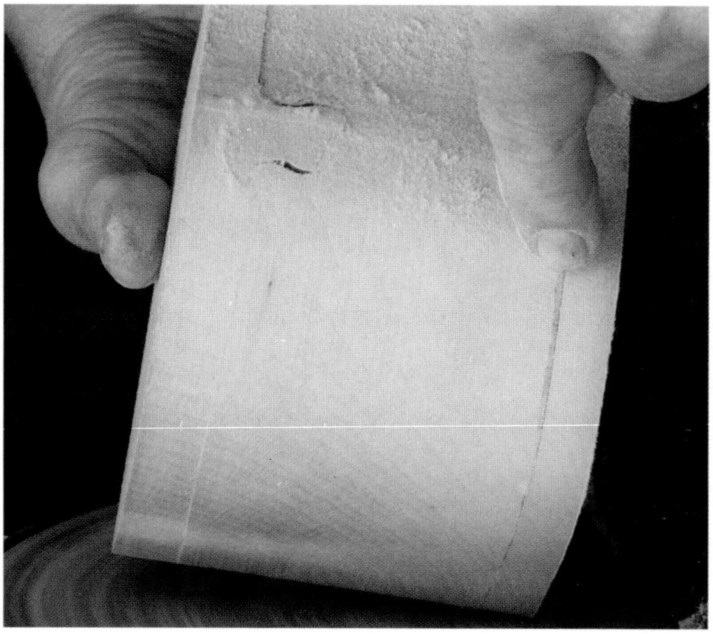

We have sanded all of the areas that need to be smoothed.

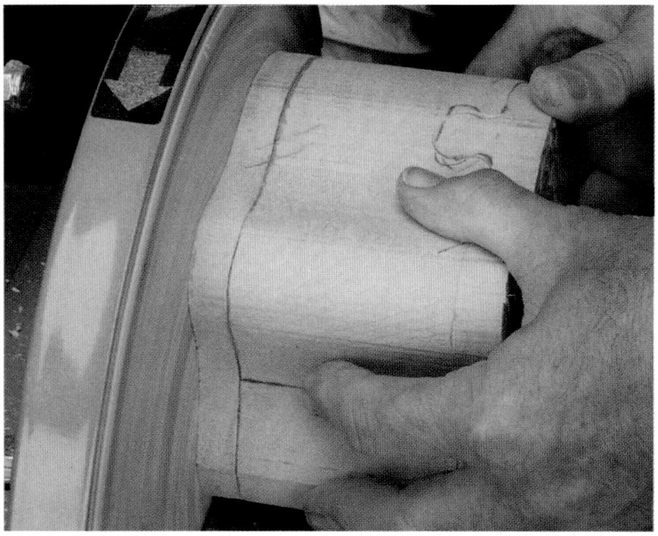

Sanding the base smooth on a disk sander using 180 grit or higher or a sheet of sandpaper of the same grit laid flat on a hard surface.

We will have to use a belt sander to reach the inside curves. We sand the outside of the box to remove all saw marks and to make sure the top and bottom match the sides exactly.

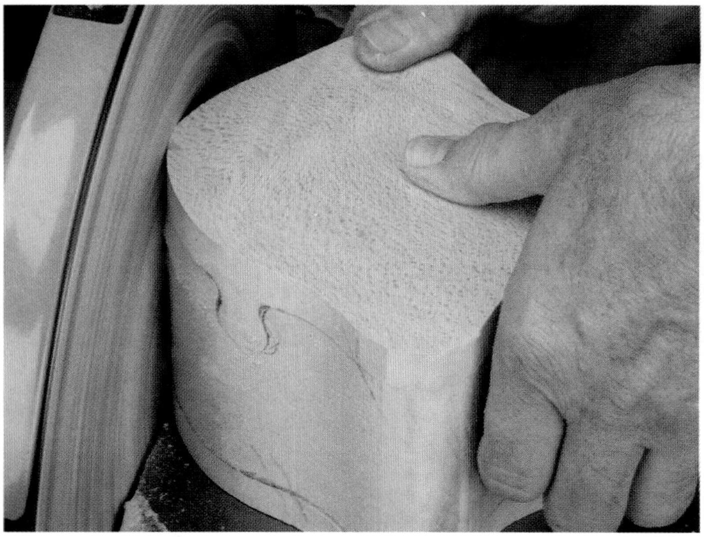

Sand the top and edges that can be reached with the disk sander to make sure that they are true and flush.

Sanding the inside of the box prior to making two small fitted interior boxes.

Cut loose the bottom of the box with the band saw.

Begin creating the two nested interior boxes by drawing on the guideline to be followed when cutting off the wood that will become the bases for these smaller boxes.

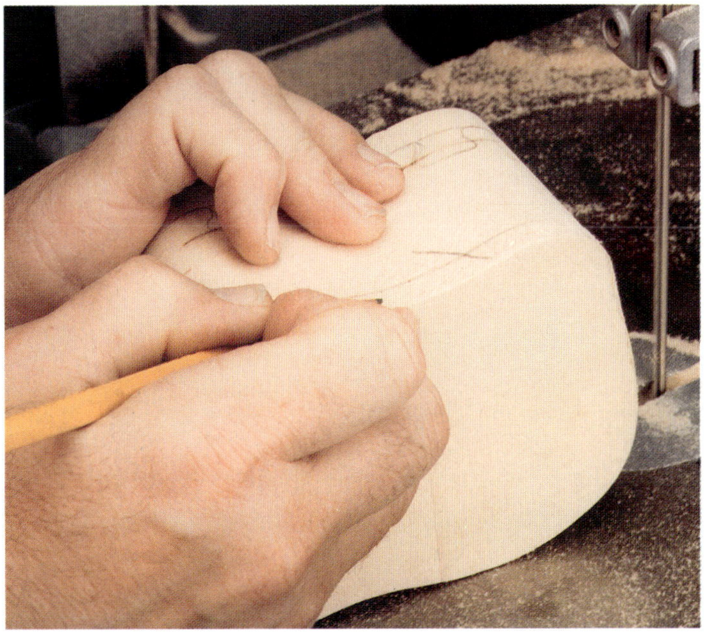

Remember to add witness lines along the base to make reassembing this piece easier.

Draw in the tops of the two interior boxes. I have decided that one of the nested box lids should lift straight off while the other should fit into a groove in the box side. The second lid slides off to one side or the other in the same manner as the larger box lid. Cut off the box tops with the band saw.

Draw in the interiors of the two small nested boxes. Note that you will not be able to cut a square corner at the point where the band saw enters each box. These corners will have to be rounded.

Enter the box with an angled cut of the saw blade. When you are done cutting out the interior you will have to back the saw blade out of the box.

The first box interior is cut out.

Rounding the corners inside of the second box. Square corners are not possible here.

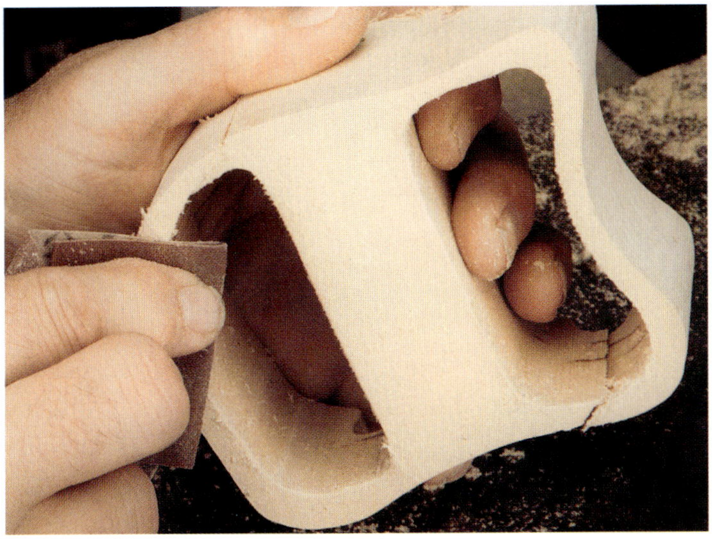

Prior to gluing the box bottom back on, sand the interior edges of the box smooth, removing rough spots and loose wood.

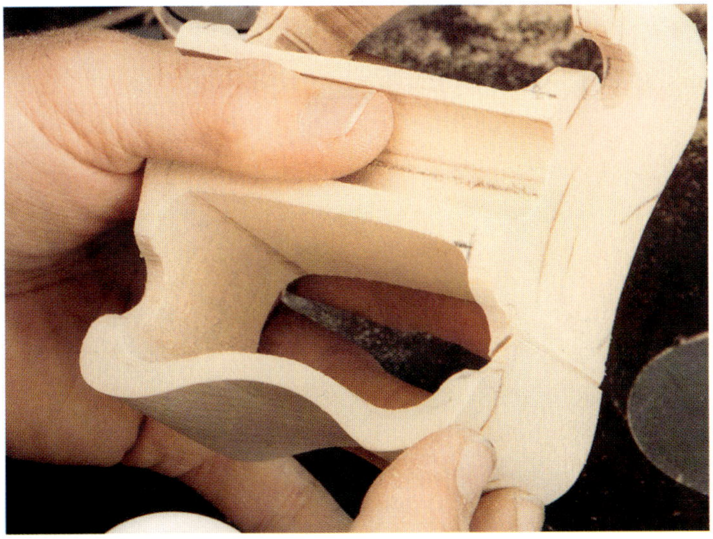

The reason for cutting into the box at an angle is to provide a larger area to glue back together when the box interior has been removed.

Seal the joints together with hot glue and use the accelerator to quickly bond the joints together.

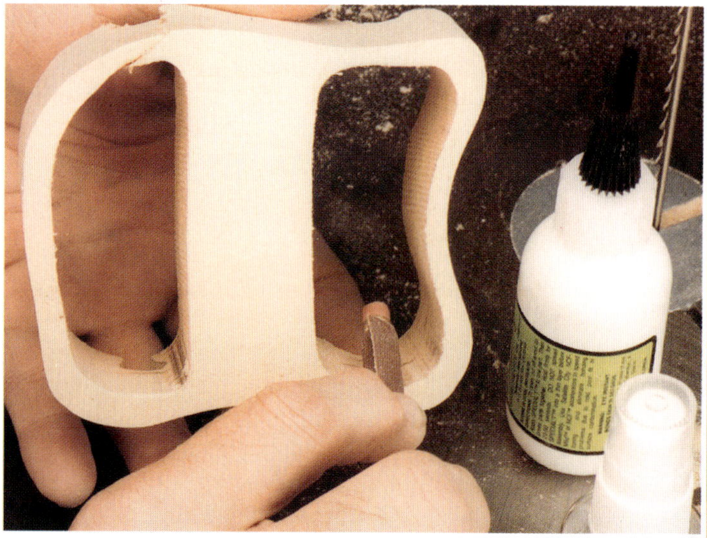

Smooth out the inside joints with sandpaper wrapped around a pencil.

Apply accelerator to the base of the box.

Prior to gluing the base back in place, match up the witness lines.

Match up the witness lines and firmly press the two pieces together to create a tight seal.

Apply the instant glue to the bottom of the box interior.

Prior to final cutting, we want to make sure that all of the inside cuts are sanded by hand.

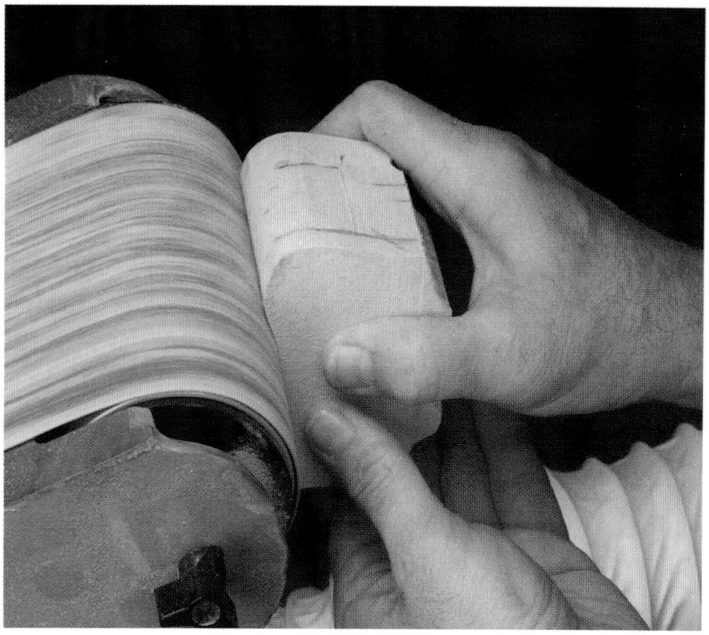

Sand the interior boxes to remove all saw marks and to make sure the lids and bases match the sides exactly.

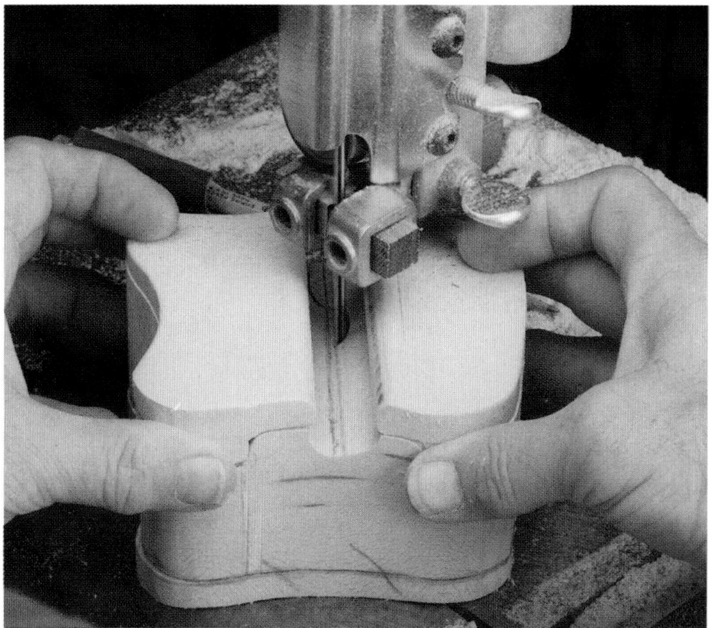

Cutting the two interior boxes loose in a wavy pattern adds to the interest of the boxes.

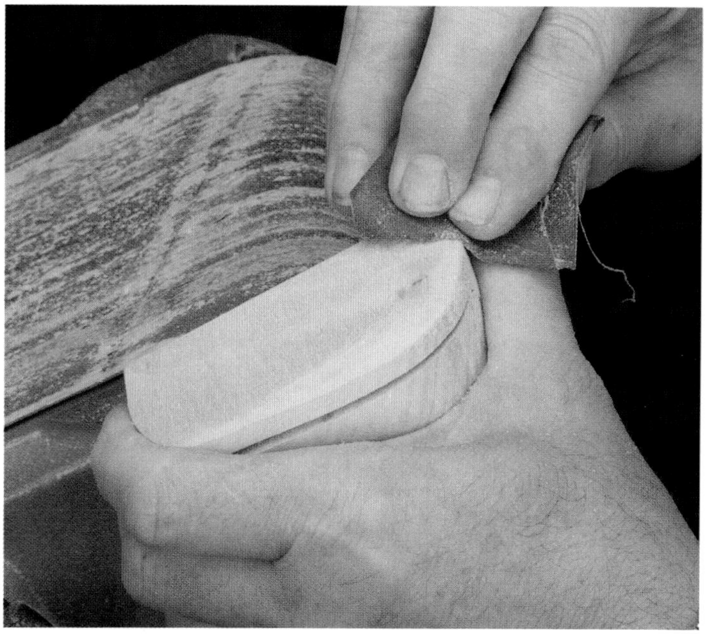

Sand the top edges of the lids round by hand.

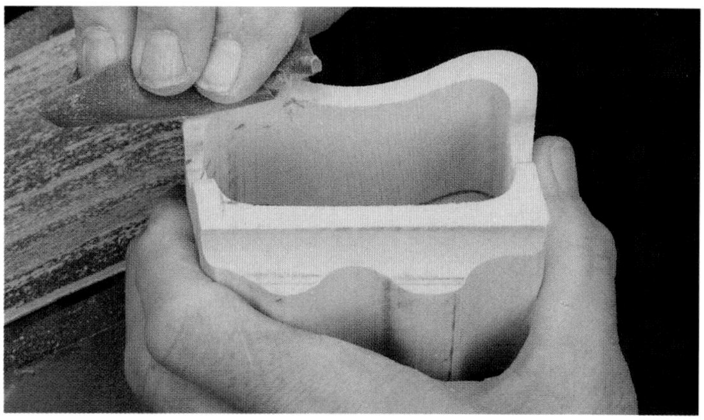

A light sanding will remove all left over pencil marks.

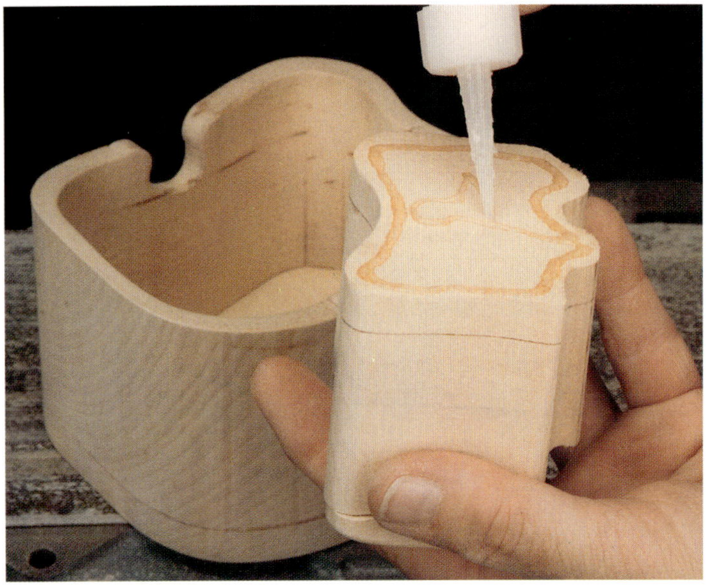

Apply quick glue to the base of the box with the lift off lid.

The other interior box has a lid designed to slide into the body of the box, allowing the box to be lifted out of the interior by the lid itself.

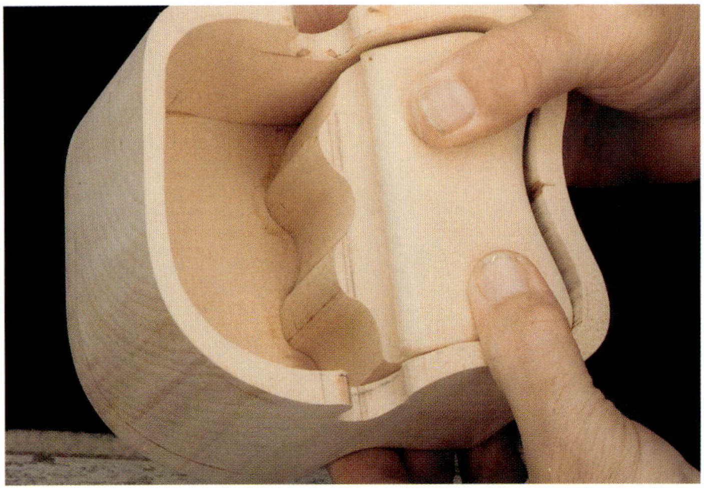

Glue the box with the lift off lid in place.

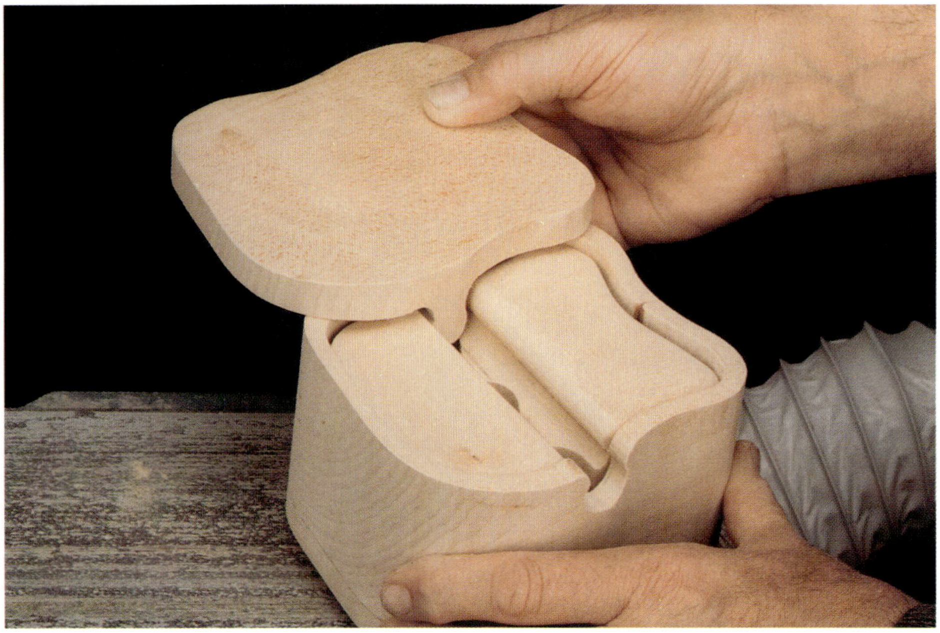

Now test the fit of all of the pieces before finishing the box.

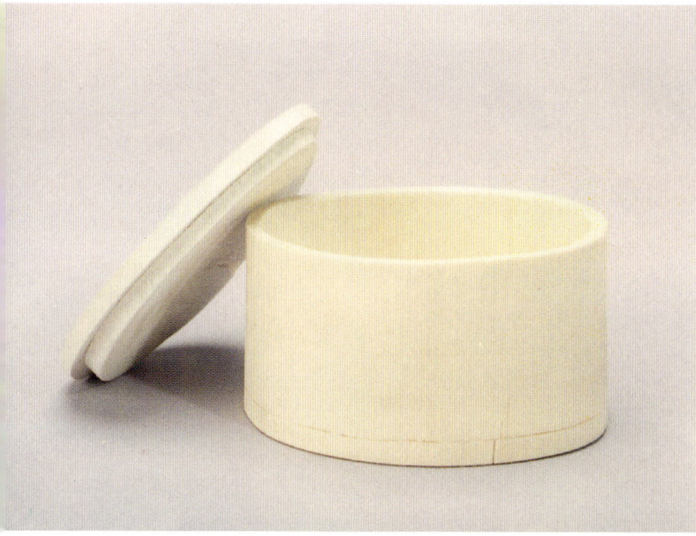

The second band saw box will be cut from a tree limb. First remove the bark from the limb with the band saw.

Use a pencil to mark in the slabs to be removed from both the box top and the bottom.

Removing both the base and top with the band saw. Set them aside.

Witness lines won't be necessary this time because the patterns in the grain make matching up the various parts simple.

Mark and cut out the interior of the box. Once again, an angled cut was made to get the saw blade into the interior of the box.

Mark and cut away a slab from the interior wood to become the inside of the box lid. Make sure to mark the top of the slab with a T so that when you glue it to the bottom of the box lid you get a tight fit.

To assemble the box top, first flip the box body upside down onto the lid. Apply accelerator to the lid's interior surface.

Seal the joint in the side of the box with the quick glue and accelerator.

Apply quick glue to the marked top surface of the inside of the box lid, making sure none of the glue is close to the outer edges.

Align the inside of the box lid properly with the sides of the box and drop it down onto the accelerator coated inside surface of the top of the box lid.

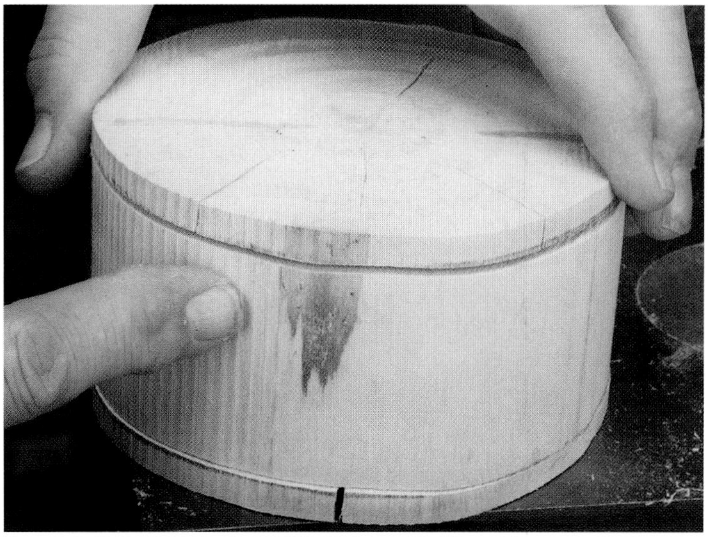

Glue the bottom of the box in place. Carefully match up the grain patterns to ensure a tight fit. Oh, by the way, the left over interior wood could now be made into another, smaller box.

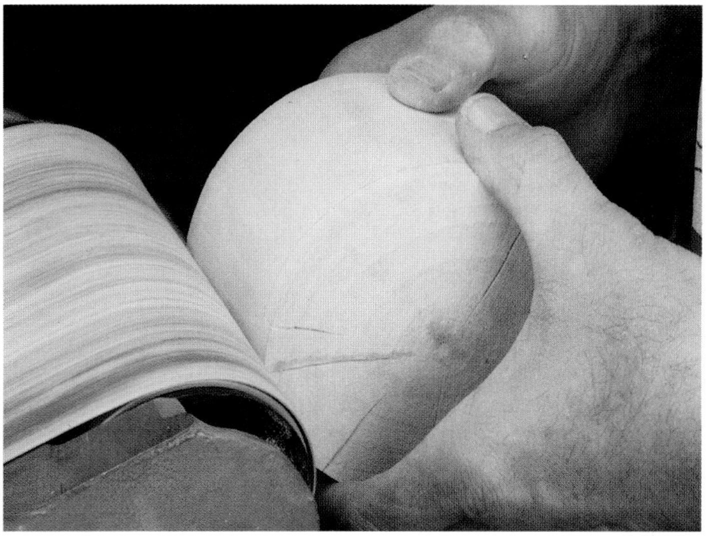

Use the sander to remove all saw marks and to refine the fit of the base and lid to the body of the box.

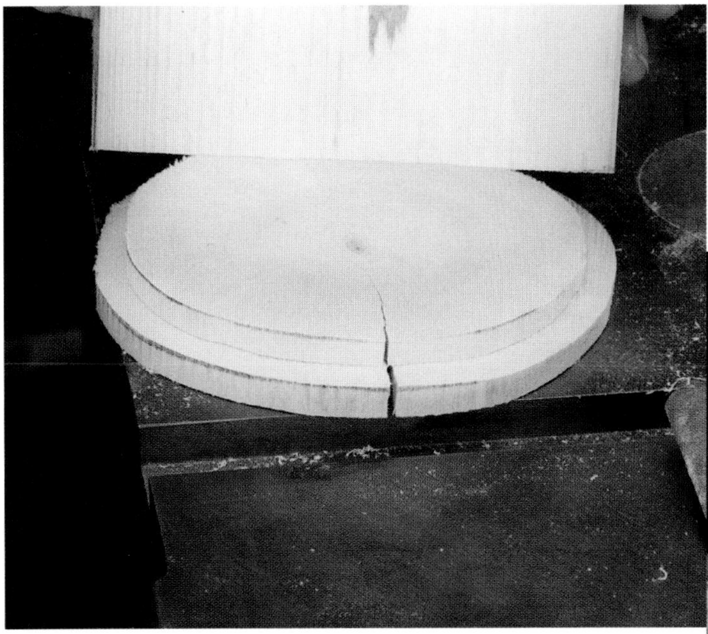

With the interior of the lid in place, the lid will fit snugly onto the box.

Also sand the tops and bottoms.

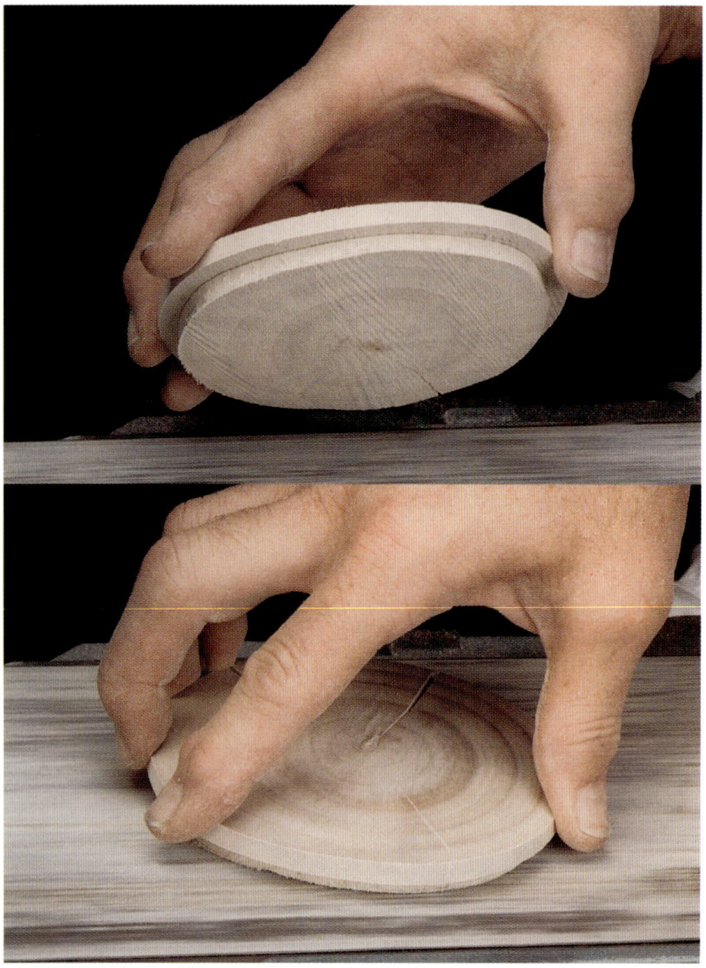

Gently sand the inside of the lid to remove any obvious saw marks.

Hand sand along the inside edge of the box to remove rough spots and pencil marks. The box is now ready for finishing.

The Log Box

Boxes may be made out of chunks of logs as well. Unusual shapes may be cut into them. First cut off what will be the back.

Lay the chunk of wood flat on the saw and make a random shaped cut for the drawer that will pull out.

Remove the center and ...

cut off the front and back.

Cut the inside shape (the drawer's interior).

Sand the edges and the inside of the drawer by hand prior to reassembly.

Using the quick glue, assemble the sides of the box drawer.

A problem develops if you cut your wood and set it aside for later assembly in warm weather ... the pieces tend to shrink and distort as you can see here.

To correct this problem, first rehydrate the wood with water.

To glue the separating pieces back together, you will want to use one of the new water activated glues. I am using Gorilla Glue. Unlike other glues, you do not have to spread Gorilla Glue out. Just lay in a line of glue and clamp the pieces together. The glue will expand to fill the void.

Glue the back of the box in place. Set the box aside until the glue has set.

After the Gorilla Glue has set, remove a thin slab from both ends of the box.

Remove the bark with the band saw.

Sand the top and bottom to level them.

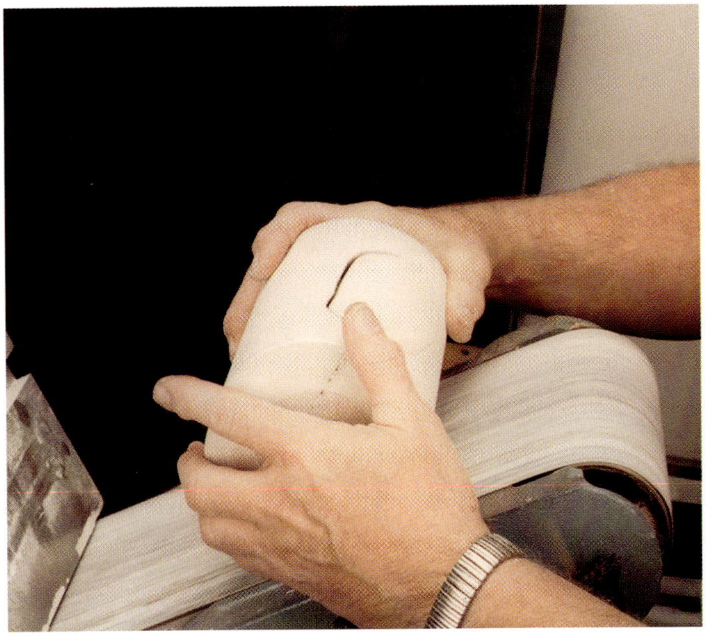

Sand the sides smooth.

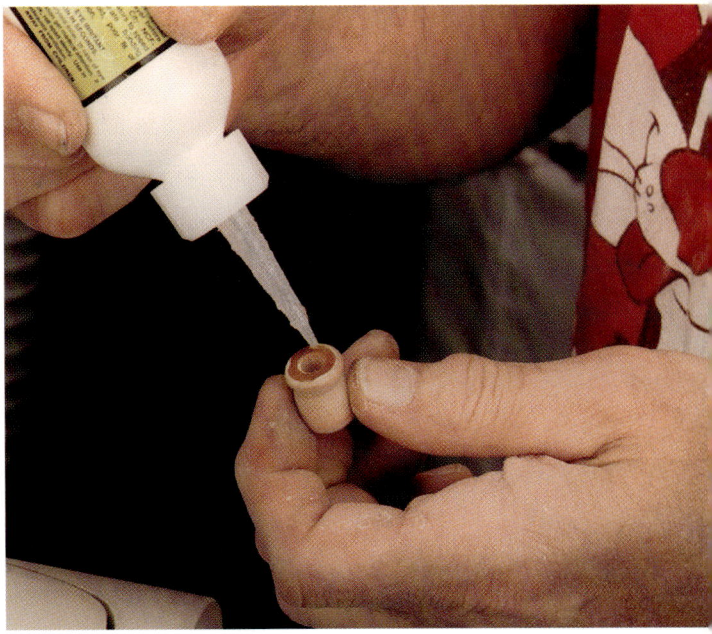

To add a knob to the drawer, first place quick setting glue on the base of the knob.

Add accelerator to the drawer front.

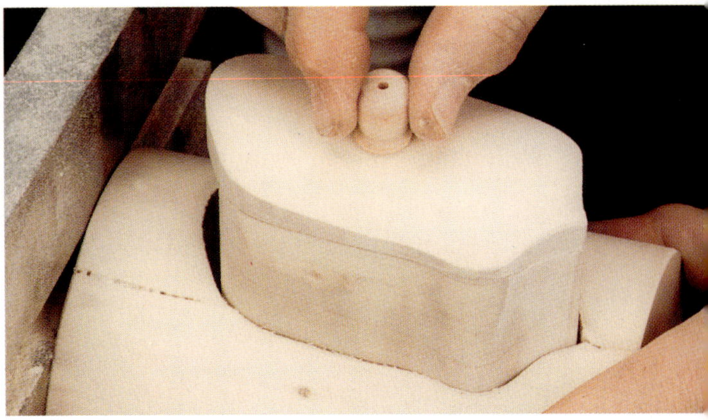

Place the knob on the drawer, hold it for a second or two, and it is firmly fixed in place. This box is ready to be finished.

Straight Mitered Cornered Boxes

An example of the straight mitered corner.

Let's move on to a straight mitered cornered box. This is an easy box to make and it has a lot of applications. Check your wood very carefully. If it is cupped in either direction, use a surface planer to straighten the wood. Remember to wear safety glasses when using the planer.

Always check to make sure that back fence is square with the table. Never take it for granted that the fence is square.

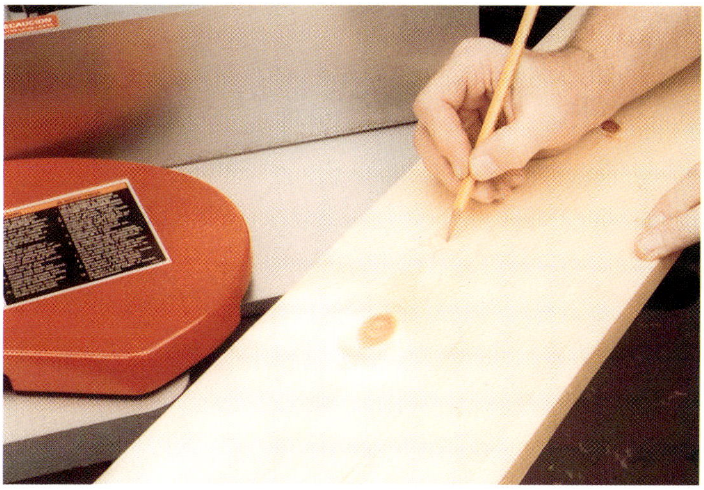

Mark the outside of the board with an "OS".

Put that outside surface against the fence. This jointer will straighten the edges with the board.

Use a wood shaper to create a nice half round on the edge of the board.

The half round shape is in place.

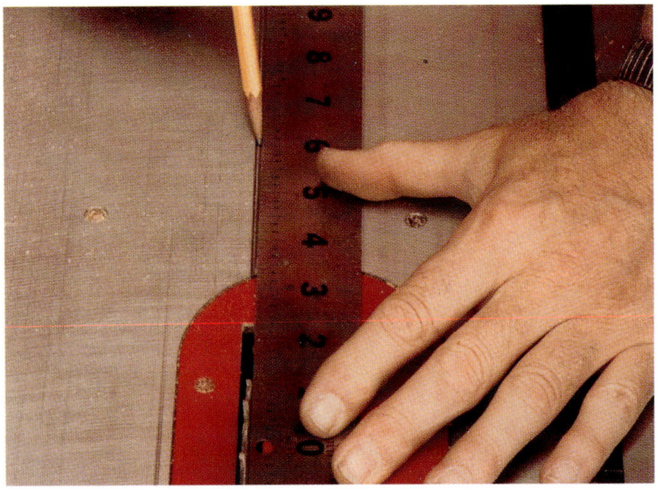

Using a straight edge, mark a line on both sides of your saw blade. This will provide you with guidelines that will sight the cuts on your boards, eliminating a lot of guess work. Please note that the blade guard has been removed on this table saw for photographic clarity only. Do not operate your power equipment with any of the safety devices removed!

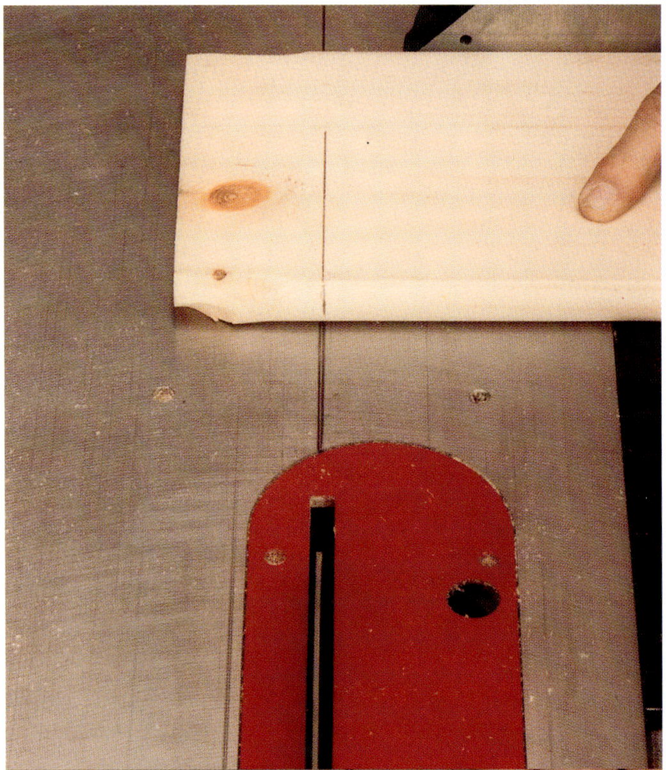

Line up the pencil mark on your board with the newly created guidelines and you will be able to push the wood through the saw blade right along the intended cut line.

Before using the table saw to cut out the sides of the box, make a sample cut and measure the kerf of the blade (the cut of the blade). This is so you will know how much extra to allow on each cut.

Now set the depth of the table saw blade at 3/8".

Place the fence at the 1/2" spacing and make a cut in the top of the board to receive a panel.

Move the fence away from the blade another 1/8" and make a cut to widen the groove. If your measurements are not exact, you might have a thin strip of wood down the middle of your groove. This is easily removed.

Repeat this process on the bottom of the box, starting with the fence 3/4" from the blade. This places the groove 3/4" from the bottom of the box. (The lower cut was a test cut in the scrap end of the board.)

Move the fence 1/8" farther away from the blade and make your second cut along the bottom of the board.

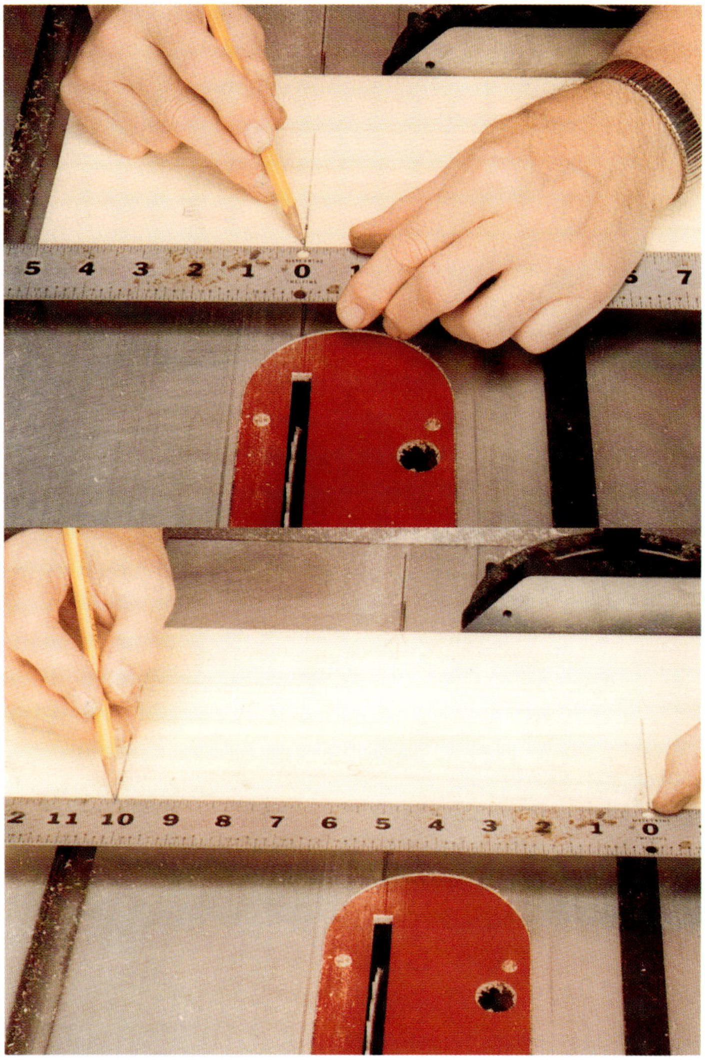

When dealing with box proportions, a good rule of thumb would be 1 x 1 x 2. The height is equal to the width of the box and the length is twice the width of the box. Our first measurement is 5" from the end, marking off the first end piece. Remember to add 1/8" from that first measured line (to account for the kerf of the saw blade) when marking off the first side piece, which measures 10 1/8".

Using the pencil marks drawn on the table saw earlier, line up your mark on the wood with the mark on the right hand side of the blade. Cut the first end piece loose.

Add 1/8" to each successive measurement. Note that the ends and sides alternate on the measured board.

Lightly number the adjoining pieces for ease of assembly later.

Now adjust the table saw blade to a 45 degree angle. It is never a good idea to put your faith entirely in the blade tilt guide. Better to check your angle with a 45 degree triangle.

Move the fence in until your end board lines up with the right hand mark on the table.

With the interior of the board facing up (note the grooves cut in earlier are facing up), cut the angle on both end pieces.

To keep the edges the same, cut both end pieces and then both side pieces (i.e. side to side and end to end). Make angled cuts along both sides as shown.

Reposition the fence to accommodate the side boards and cut the angles again. Remember to align the end of the board with the right hand mark on the table.

Turn the side boards around and make your next cuts.

To check your cuts, first line the pieces up against the table saw fence in order.

Apply a strip of masking tape along both the top and bottom of the boards, holding them together.

Using the tape as a hinge, simply roll the box pieces up and tape the box together. The box fits together well.

Reset the blade to 90 degrees, using a right angle triangle to check between the teeth that the blade is properly set.

Next set the guide fence to a measurement of 4 1/16" and cut the boards for width.

Set the fence at 9 1/16" to begin cutting the top and bottom boards for size. Make your cuts.

Now set the fence for 3/8". Then set the height of the blade for 3/8". Run all four sides of the top and bottom boards through the saw at this setting.

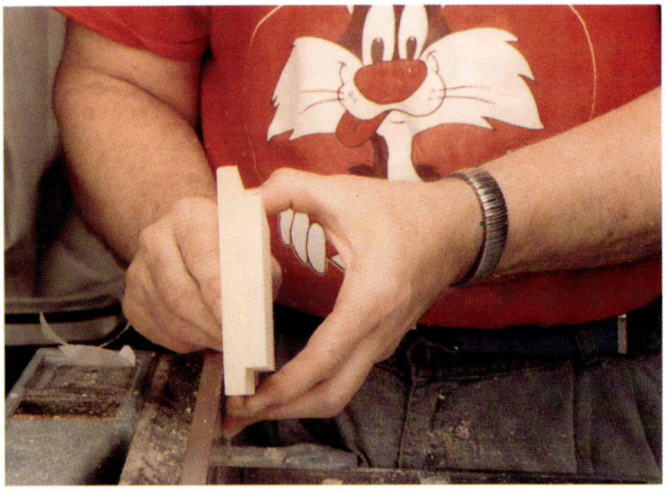

Without moving the fence, turn the boards up on end with the saw cuts visible to you and cut again. This starts to create the lip that will fit into the sides of the box.

Set the fence 1/8" closer to the blade and rerun the same cut again, reducing the lip to 3/16". This lip will now fit into the grooves cut into the box sides.

Now dry fit the box to test for size.

The box fits together!

Use yellow carpenter's glue to assemble the box. Place the carpenter's glue on the joints themselves. Spread the glue along all of the edges.

If you are working in a warm climate, you must move right along when applying the glue because it will set quicker. Fit the box together again.

Once the box is together, make sure all the joints fit tightly. Wipe away excess glue with a damp cloth. Wrap masking tape around the box at the top and bottom and set it aside to dry. We will discuss cutting box lids and attaching hinges later.

Straight Mitered Cornered Boxes with False Finger Joints

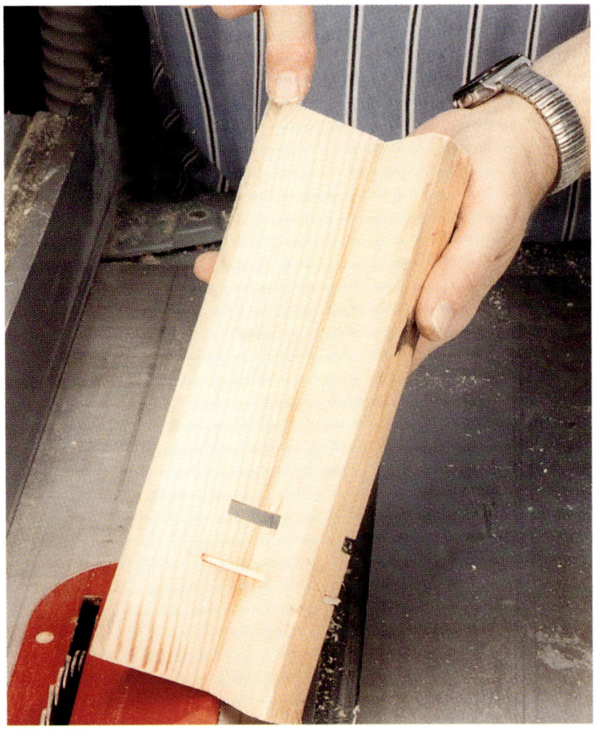

This jig makes false finger joints. Take a 2 x 4, split it at a 45 degree angle, place the two halves edge to edge as shown, and glue a piece of hard board to the bottom, holding the two halves in place and creating a V shaped trough. After the glue is set, first run the jig through the saw to cut a kerf all the way through and place a key in the kerf. Raise the saw blade so it protrudes past the jig half the distance of the wood used in the box. Move the blade over the distance you want your finger joints to be set apart and make another cut of the size you want for your false joint inserts.

False finger joints.

This type of joint is used with the standard miter joint. Place the edge of the box in the jig and run it through the blade. A word of advice, do not put your hand against the jig to push or you might accidentally place a finger in line with blade. Keep your hands on the box to move it forward, with those fingers well away from the blade

Index the box over, placing the newly cut false joint over the key, and cut again. Progress down the side of the box. Repeat this process along all four corners.

Cut splines to fit into the false joints.

The cuts are in place.

Now place carpenter's glue in the kerf cut.

Insert the splines into the false joints, making sure the splines are overextended on both sides.

Using a flush cutting saw with a flexible blade, cut the splines flush with the surface of the box. This step eliminates the need for a lot of sanding.

Rough cut the splines, shortening their lengths.

Do a little minor sanding on the newly completed false finger joints.

When cutting the lid from the box with the false finger joints, make sure to leave at least one joint in the lid section. To remove the lid, first set your saw blade to 90 degrees. Next, take a piece of wood from the same material you have been cutting and use it as a height gauge to set the blade to within approximately 1/32" of the thickness of the board. Cut the lid on all sides, with 1/32" to spare. A razor blade or a utility knife will finish cutting the box lid loose. Not cutting clear through the box walls with the table saw blade prevents the lid from closing as you cut and binding the blade.

The hinges are now in place.

Use masking tape to orient the lid and box correctly and hold them in place prior to putting the hinges on. Make sure that the hinges are located the same distance in from each side. Also make sure that the hinges are square. When working with small screws, it is best if you have a sharp awl or some other small instrument with which to make small guide holes to begin the screws.

Mitered Joint with Spline Boxes

Here is an example of the mitered joint with spline that we will make next.

Next, place one of the sides you have cut for your box against the angled 2 x 4.

The second mitered joint we will explore is a mitered joint with splines. The splines add strength. Our first step is to cut our mitered joints in the same way as before. The second step involves producing a jig to make the spline cuts in the joints. The first step in making the jig (shown here) is to take a 2 x 4 and cut it at a 45 degree angle.

Assemble the jig by fastening two small scraps of lumber to the 2 x 4 with screws.

Now, set your fence at 3 1/2", your blade at 1/8", insert your box side piece into the jig with the miter cut facing down to the blade, and cut the spline joint (completed spline joint shown here). Cut all eight ends this way.

Now we have to cut the splines themselves. Set the saw blade at 90 degrees. Then cut your board to 1/2" in width.

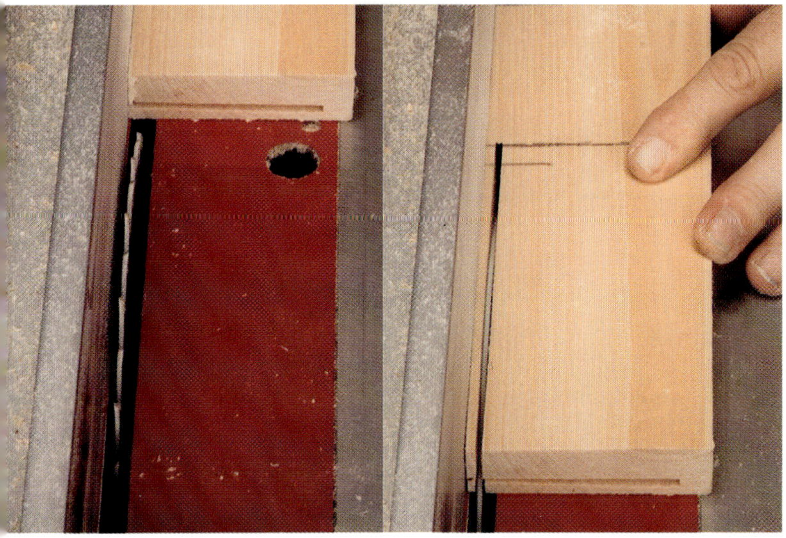

We need to cut 1/8" strips off the board to create the splines. Set the fence to 1/8" from the blade and make your first cut. You do not want to cut all the way down the board or your 1/8" thick splines will drop through the gap to the floor below. Only cut away as much as you need, leaving each spline attached to the board.

Move the fence 1/4" farther away from the blade and cut again (this distance takes into account the 1/8" kerf of the blade itself).

Keep moving the fence back 1/4" until you have cut four splines from the 2x4. I usually cut a few extra for future use.

Cut the splines loose from the 2x4 and they are ready for use.

We are going to cut rabbet joints in the top and bottom. To set the height of the band saw blade, use a piece of scrap wood the same thickness as the sides of the box.

Here is the rabbet joint. It is made following the same steps used to create the lip for the box lid and base we have already completed.

Dry fit the box. Measure the width and depth of the box.

To glue the spline box joints together, first place carpenter' s glue down into the spline joint. Then spread glue across the miter joint as well.

Place the splines in the joints and begin assembling the box.

Clamp the walls of the box together. Glue both the top and bottom lids in place, clamp them together, and set the box aside to dry.

Finger Joint Boxes

Finger joints.

Let's move along to finger joints. For these we will need a dado head. When you are assembling your dado head, make sure that you offset the chippers in a staggered line, one just behind the other.

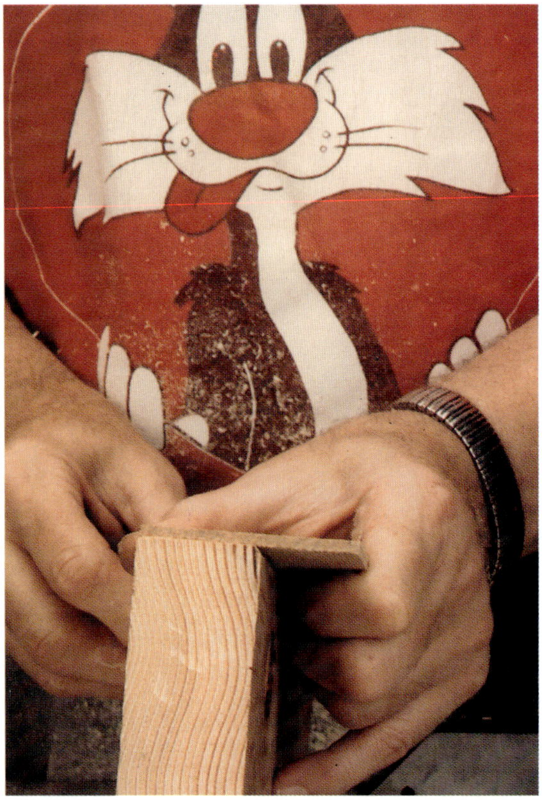

To make a jig for the finger joints, first glue a piece of hard board to the the bottom of a 1 x 6 board. Cutting a dado through the boards.

Locate exactly where the second dado cut should be by using a piece of wood the box is made from as a spacer between the dado blade and the index point. Now, cut a second dado (this took two tries as you can see), making sure to hold the template firmly against the mitre gauge while cutting.

Cut a piece of wood to fit the dado. Glue it in place so that the wood will act as an index point.

Do not move the jig just yet. Shut the saw off and attach the jig to the miter gauge with two screws.

Time to test the jig. For your first dado cut, the board should be firmly against the inner edge of the index pin. Make your dado cuts, moving down the board, each previous cut fitting over the index pin before the next cut is made. Run some test pieces to check the calibration of your jig and the depth of the cut. If we end up with a situation like this, the blade has not been set quite high enough.

If your joints are too loose, like this, move the jig away from the blade and cut another test joint. If your joints are too tight, you move the jig in the opposite direction.

Once properly adjusted, this is the way your joints should fit.

Lay your box walls out side by side and mark the adjoining joints with the same number so that they can be properly matched later (Ex. where board 1 and 2 meet, mark each board with the number 1, where board 2 and 3 meet, mark each board 2, and so on.)

Move the board over, placing the first cut over the index pin with the board hard against the inside edge of the pin and make your second cut. Continue moving across the board in this manner.

To make the dado joint, first place your board hard against the index pin and cut.

When you finish your last cut on the first board, place the next board against it and make the first cut on your next board. This will keep the joints properly aligned. Then keep moving the board to the index pin.

Using the dado, make a rabbet cut along the top and bottom edges of each box side panel.

Dry fit the finger joint box. Do not worry about the gaps at the top and bottom edges of the joints. They will be filled in later.

You can use the dado head to trim the excess wood from the box lid.

Use the dado to cut a rabbet around the edge of the box lid.

Test fit the lid and repeat this process to create the box bottom.

Prepare to cut the pins to fill the gaps in the finger joint ends. Use the dado blade to cut wood down to the appropriate size.

Use a push stick when cutting these pins to keep your fingers well clear of the dado.

These pins have been cut to size and are ready to be cut for length and inserted into the gaps at the ends of the finger joints.

One of the gaps in the finger joints to be filled with the pins. These gaps only occur on the end boards of the box walls.

Apply carpenter's glue to the finger joints and spread it evenly with a brush.

Join the finger joints together and insert a pin into a gap at the end.

Clamp the glued joints together.

Cut away the excess pin wood filling the finger joint gaps with a flush cutting saw.

To add a decorative touch, cut the very corners of the box at a 45 degree angle.

The gaps in the joints are filled and cut flush.

Use a sacrificial board to protect your fence while cutting all of the edges off at 45 degrees.

Use carpenter's glue and clamps to join the top and bottom lids to the box.

The corners have been cut.

Once again, to remove the lid, first set your blade to 90 degrees. Next, take a piece of wood from the same material you have been cutting and use it as a height gauge to set the blade to within approximately 1/32" of the thickness of the board.

Place witness lines on the box to keep the lid oriented in the proper position for the remainder of the project.

Remove the wood and determine how big you want your lid to be. I have set my fence at 1 3/4" from the blade.

The lid is cut on all sides, with 1/32" to spare. A razor blade or a utility knife will finish cutting the box lid loose. Not cutting clear through the box walls with the table saw blade prevents the lid from closing as you cut and binding the blade.

With the witness lines in place, use either a razor blade or a utility knife to separate the lid from the box body and remove the small amount of excess wood that remains.

This box is now ready for finishing.

This method for removing the lid will work with all of your boxes.

Finishing the Boxes

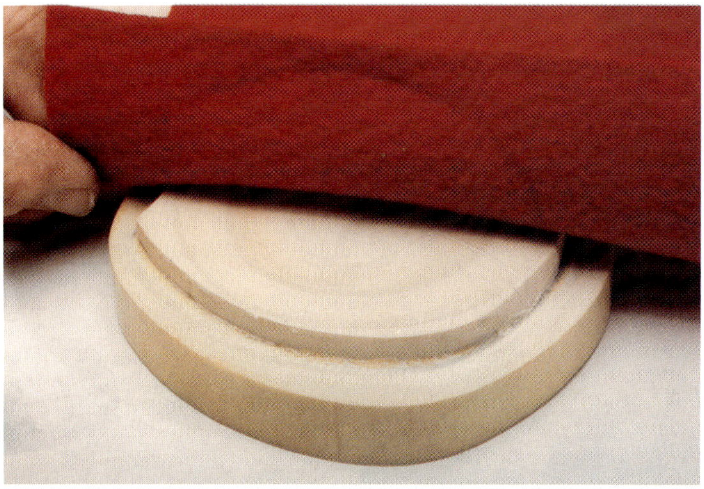

To line the interior of a box with felt, first lay the felt over the insert on the inside lid of the box.

Next, trace the outline of the lid insert onto the felt. The inside of the lid matches the shape of the base within the box. Cut out the felt along the traced lines and insert the felt into the bottom of the box for a test fitting. We will fix the felt in place permanently later.

A scrap piece of lumber with a square end is good enough to transfer the depth of the box interior to a sheet of paper. Transfer the measurement from the wood to the paper along its length.

Cut out the strip of paper and fit it into the inside of the box. This way we will be able to mark the length of the box interior. Cut off the excess paper and you have created a paper guide.

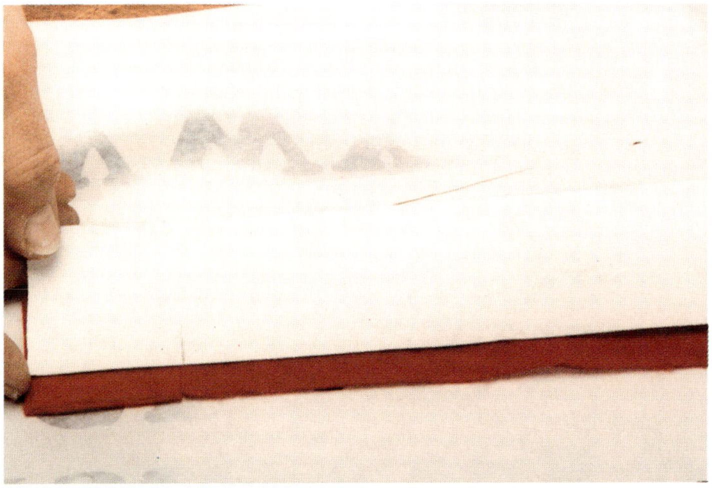

Use the paper guide to cut the right amount of felt to line the box wall. The felt is cut.

Use a spray adhesive to coat the inside of the box.

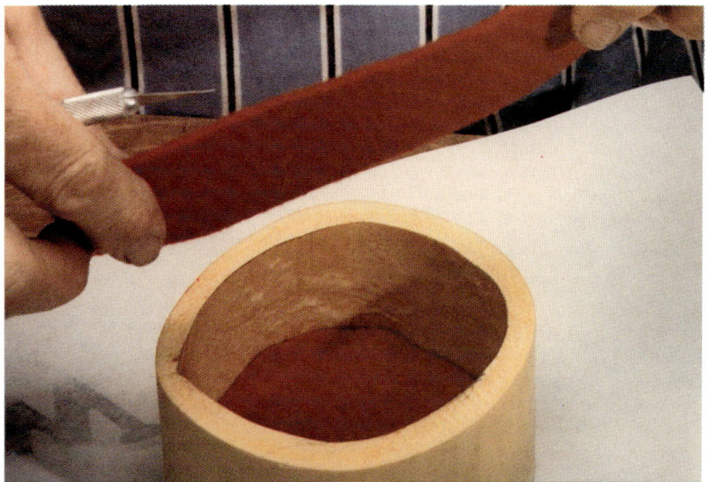

Insert the felt and cut off any excess.

The same technique works even when placing felt within this multi-sided sewing box. With this sewing box, the sides are the lenght you would like them and the end cuts of each board are at 22 1/2 degrees. Make dado cuts in the sides for the top and bottom boards.

When you are finished with your box, don't forget to sign it. A nice finishing touch is to add small felt pads to the base. This way the box won't mar furniture and people tend to feel the box is truly complete with these in place.

Spray the box with a clear wood finish.

Buff the clear spray down with a very fine sandpaper. The buffing process will bring out the true beauty of the wood.

Another way to apply a finish is to cut up a paint roller into various sized pieces and use them as applicators.

For this sewing box, I'm using a Minwax stain and sealer. While the color is Ebony, this is a very thin stain, it does not give a solid coat. Use one of the small rollers to apply the stain.

Applying the Ebony stain to the box lid. Let the stain dry. Once dried, continue applying coats until you achieve the desired color.

Anything can be used for legs, even small wooded pieces meant for drawer pulls.

Apply felt pads to the bottoms of the legs as a finishing touch.

I'm using Minwax Red Mahogany to finish this miter and spline joint box, both inside and out.

Once the box is stained, set it aside to dry. You do not have to put a smooth finish on with this stain. Heavily stained areas are not a problem as they will appear to be wood grain variations.

Using the Red Mahogany again to give this pure white holly wood more interest.

This box, with rabbet joints, features saw created decorations. These were made by running the saw blade along the body at different intervals.

The bottom piece is cut away with the band saw to form legs.

I used a standard black enamel on this box, both inside and out. Once dried, we will antique it with gold antiquing which will make the details stand out.

The gold antique glaze has been brushed on with the cut rollers. Wait for three hours after the base coat is applied before adding the glaze. Wipe excess glaze off to achieve the desired effect. After the stains have dried, you may apply a clear coat finish.

On this example (a mitered joint box with a small decorative groove cut around it with the saw blade) we used finishing wax to seal the surface and bring out the color of the wood.

Gallery

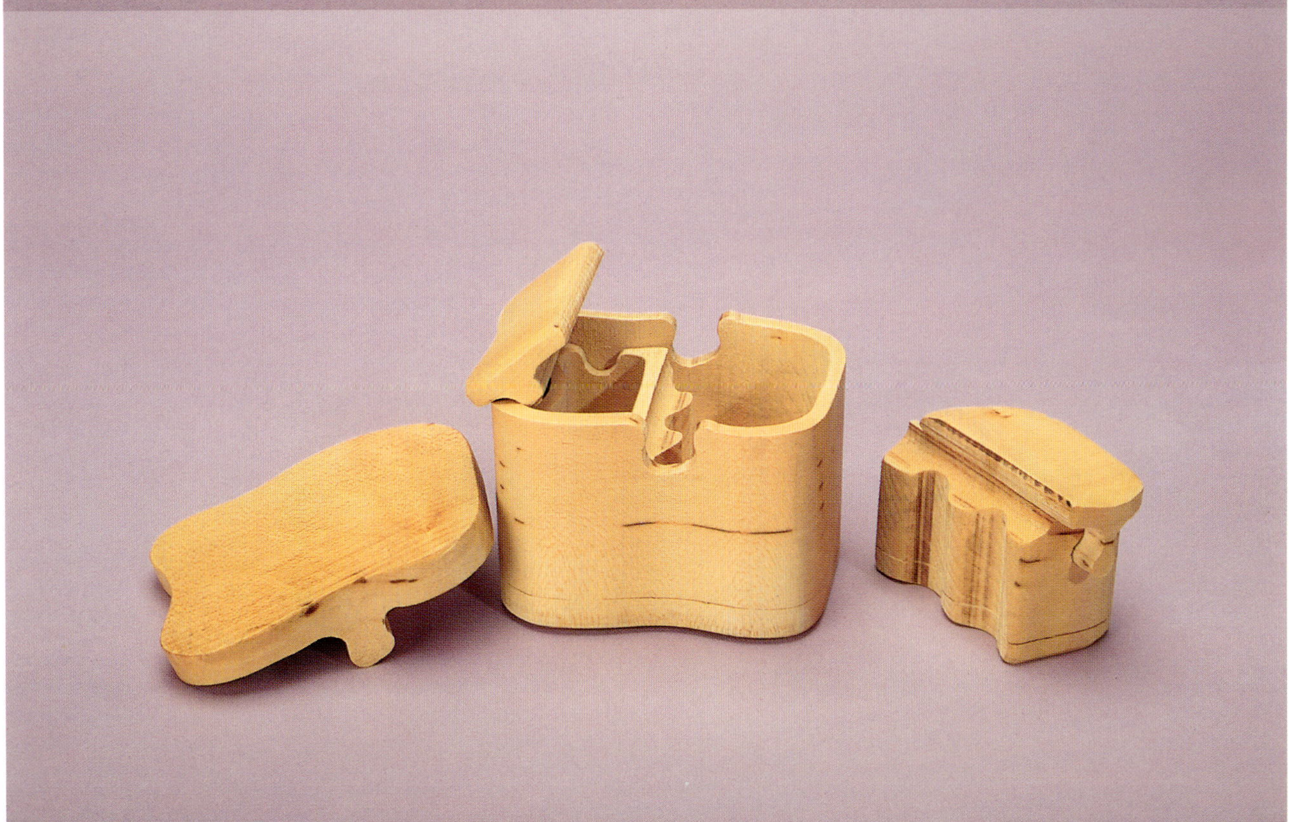

More Titles from Schiffer Publishing

Do-It-Yourself Coffins for Pets and People Dale Power, *Text written with and photography by Jeffrey B. Snyder*. Dale Power departs from his usual animal carvings, burying himself in a new art form—the manufacture of special boxes for pets and people. Here's one project you won't want to put off till tomorrow. All of the tools and techniques needed to produce strong and beautiful coffins are presented here in clear, concise language. Color photographs illustrate every step in the construction of three pet-size and three human-size coffins. Detailed patterns are provided and different box construction techniques are revealed. One box design even doubles as a beautiful blanket chest or coffee table. Once the coffins are built, the discussion turns to the many moldings, appliques, linings, and finishes which may be used to make each coffin unique. A color gallery is also provided. With full color illustrations and detailed instructions, this book is a challenge to the novice and a joy for the experienced craftsman.

Size: 8 1/2" x 11"	200+ color photos/6 patterns	64pp.
ISBN: 0-7643-0337-6	soft cover	$14.95

Finishes for Wood Dale Power, *Text written with and photography by Jeffrey B. Snyder*. Here's a step-by-step finishing school, featuring 14 different techniques for refining your wood surfaces. All of the tools and methods needed to successfully change the image of any wooden surface are provided. More than 200 color photographs accompany the text. In addition, there are instructions for restoring damaged finishes. The projects are arranged in order, from the most basic to the very advanced, and a color gallery provides a final look at all of the finishes. This book is an invaluable resource for everyone wishing to finish their wood up right.

Size: 8 1/2" x 11"	200+ color photos	64 pp.
ISBN: 0-7643-0338-4	soft cover	$14.95

Useful Beauty: Turning Practical Items on a Wood Lathe Dick Sing, *Photography by and text written with Alison Levie*. Dick Sing has directed his creative wood turning skills to the design of six attractive projects with variations. Three variations of bottle stoppers and decorative jar lids can transform the practical into the beautiful. The weed vase and the small mirror can make charming gifts; the spinning top and baby rattle will delight any young child. Instructions for each project along with step-by-step photographs make these fun projects easy to learn and fun to do. Variations provide a challenge for the more experienced turners,and a gallery with numerous examples encourages the adventurous to experiment.

Size: 8 1/2" x 11"	250 color photos	64 pp.
ISBN: 0-88740-851-6	soft cover	$12.95

Wood Lathe Projects for Fun and Profit Dick Sing, *Text written with and photography by Alison Levie*. Wood speaks to Dick Sing. With his skill as a woodturner, and his keen understanding of both the lathe and the wood, Dick has created a number of projects which offer something a little different. In this new book, he leads the turner through four projects which are easy enough for the beginner and fun enough for someone with experience. They also are very successful at craft shows. With step-by-step instructions illustrated with clear full-color photographs, he helps the turner discover the shape of a delightful little clock holder in a piece of wood and turn out a finished piece which would add character to any desk or table. He also provides instructions for a candle dish, a desk set with a base, a pen, and a letter opener, and a bookmark. Each project is covered completely, including numerous tips on style and finishing techniques, and a knowledge of wood, including some exotic woods which make striking finished projects.

Size: 8 1/2" x 11" 250 color Photos 64 pp.
ISBN: 0-88740-675-0 soft cover $12.95

Hewing Contemporary Bowls Rip & Tammi Mann, *Text written with and photography by Douglas Congdon-Martin*. With step-by-step, fully illustrated instructions, the authors lead the craftsperson to a beautiful handhewn octagonal bowl. In the gallery are a variety of contemporary bowls that can be made using the same techniques, though some will require the skill that comes from experience. They include octagonal bowls, bowls in the shapes of states, and bowls with natural exteriors. Rip and Tammi use only hand tools, the bowl adze, a bowl shave and a carver's hook. They begin with a blank and conclude with an oil finish process that makes the bowls beautiful and perfectly safe for use with food. Each step is illustrated in color, with a complete description of design and technique concerns. Both the beginner and the experienced woodworker will enjoy the creation of these functional, beautiful pieces.

Size: 8 1/2" x 11" 250 step-by-step color photos/Gallery 64 pp.
ISBN: 0-88740-710-2 soft cover $12.95

Basic Bowl Turning with Judy Ditmer Judy Ditmer. In this full color, beautiful new work, Judy Ditmer shares her extensive knowledge of bowl turning with the novice turner. Beginning with the preparation and seasoning of the bowl blank, Judy takes the turner step-by-step through the finished product. Along the way she covers the proper use of tools, design considerations, and safety considerations for the turner. The techniques she shares will have an immediate impact on the readers understanding and practice of woodturning. While addressed particularly to those who are new to turning, Judy's years of experience come through and will be valuable to turners of all levels. The project in the book is a beautiful salad bowl. Step-by-step photographs cover the process from beginning to end, including the construction of necessary jigs for the lathe. A gallery will spark the imagination of the reader and begin to reveal the possibilities of turning.

Size: 8 1/2" x 11" 250+ color photos 64 pp.
ISBN: 0-88740-627-0 soft cover $12.95